How
My
Family
Lives
in
America

Susan Kuklin

ALADDIN PAPERBACKS

The author would like to thank the families who participated in this book:
Daisy Curbeon and Dominique Sengane Dieng,
their children, Sanu and Badu, and their extended family;
Milta Zeno and Nester A. Cruz,
their son, Eric Anthony, and their friends and family;
Michel Chen and Yuan Lee, their children, April, Julius, and May;
and the children of the Columbia Chinese school.
The author very much appreciates the help of the following people:
my editor, Sharon Steinhoff, Magatte Kebe, Bumou Wane, Theodora Laurie, Nack Waxman,
Serge Gavronsky, Jeff Segall, Fran Katzman, Grace T. E. Ooi, Betty Eng, and Dorothy Li,
and the Chinese Saturday School at Columbia University.

First Aladdin Paperbacks edition September 1998

Aladdin Paperbacks
An imprint of Simon & Schuster
Children's Publishing Division
1230 Avenue of the Americas
New York, NY 10020

The text of this book is set in 16-point Bembo
Book design by Jo Anne Metsch

Printed in Hong Kong

10 9 8 7 6 5 4

The Library of Congress has cataloged the hardcover edition as follows:
Kuklin, Susan. How my family lives in America / Susan Kuklin. — 1st ed.   p.   cm.
Summary: African-American, Asian-American, and Hispanic-American
children describe their families' cultural traditions.
ISBN 0-02-751239-8
1. Minorities—United States—Social life and customs—Juvenile literature.
2. Afro-Americans—Social life and customs—Juvenile literature.
3. Asian Americans—Social life and customs—Juvenile literature.
4. Hispanic Americans—Social life and customs—Juvenile literature.
5. United States—Social life and customs—1971—Juvenile literature.
[1. Afro-Americans—Social life and customs. 2. Asian Americans—Social life and customs.
3. Hispanic Americans—Social life and customs.] I. Title.
E184.A1K85 1992   305.8'00973—dc20   91-22949
ISBN 0-689-82221-9 (Aladdin pbk.)

dedicated to
my Russian–American grandparents,
Sarah and Meyer Gussman

Sanu, Eric, and April are American children with families just like yours. They have parents, grandparents, aunts, and uncles who love them and take care of them. Year after year, their families celebrate special days together in special ways. Because Sanu, Eric, and April each have at least one parent who did not grow up in the United States, their family heritage is an interesting mixture. Some traditions, remembered from a parent's childhood in another place, are kept alive in America. And sometimes, with the help of Sanu, Eric, and April, new traditions are started.

Here are their stories.

My name is Sanu. A long time ago, Sanu was a princess in Africa. My brother, Badu, was named after a famous warrior. He's glad about that.

We have these names because my daddy was born in Senegal, a country far away in West Africa. He moved to America to go to college. My *maam bou djigen* (mahm boo deejen) and *maam bou gor* (mahm boo gore), which means "daddy's mommy" and "daddy's daddy" in a language people speak in Senegal, still live there. When we visited them last year, I learned all about the Senegalese part of me. I learned to call Mommy *Yay* (yań ee) and Daddy *Bay* (bań ee). *Maam bou djigen* and *Maam bou gor* gave Badu a drum and African clothing. He dresses African style every chance he gets.

I have an American grandmother, too.
She lives in a city called Baltimore, where my
mother grew up. My mommy's mommy
comes to visit us in New York City on
weekends. Then she teaches me about good
manners, about being neat and clean, about
standing straight and tall.

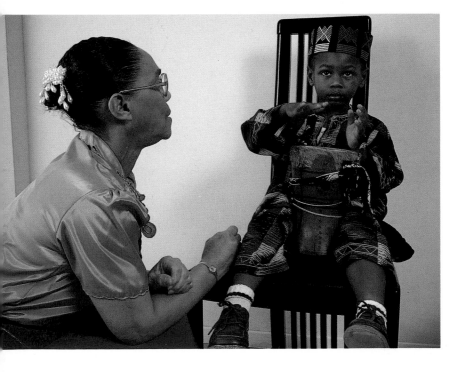

Grandma sings to us the songs she taught
Mommy. Our favorites are "Precious Lord
Take My Hand" and "Hush Little Baby
Don't You Cry." When Badu tries to play
along on his African drum, it doesn't sound
like Africa.

During the week, I go to Mommy's work after school to help out. The thing I like about my mommy's hairdressing shop is that it reminds me of how people look in Senegal. In my daddy's village, the girls weave a kind of cloth into their braid. This is called a Senegalese twist. I'm only five, so I'm still learning how to make a regular braid.

Sometimes Daddy picks me up after his work and takes me shopping for food. Daddy knows how to cook African style. Together we buy carrots, cabbage, eggplant, tomatoes, yams, and cassava, a vegetable that is like a potato.

Daddy likes to tease Mommy. "In Africa the wife gets the food and cooks it, too."

"You're in America now," my mommy says, laughing.

For a special meal my daddy fixes *tiebou dienn* (chéb-oo-jenn) for lunch, just like his family has in Senegal. *Tiebou dienn* is rice and fish and vegetables. For this meal, we invite my daddy's relatives, Fifi, Sambo, and Hussane, to join us.

Before we eat, we all wash our hands the way we did in my father's village. I want everyone to hurry up.

"In Africa," my father says, "the children must be patient and wait their turn."

"You're in America now," I giggle.

At this meal, everyone dresses like people do in Senegal. We put a cloth on the floor, not on the table, since it is the custom to eat on the ground in Senegal. Everyone eats together from one big bowl. Here's the best part: we get to eat with our hands, not with forks and spoons.

Daddy shows us how to squeeze the oil out of the *tiebou dienn*. While we eat, we hear stories about our parents when they were little in Senegal and in Baltimore. Mommy says how lucky we are to be African Americans.

My name is Eric. I live in a tall apartment building in New York City with my mommy and daddy and our pet parrot called Pepí.

My daddy and all my grandparents came to New York from Puerto Rico. Daddy showed me how to find Puerto Rico on a map. It is an island in the ocean not too far from Florida. Mommy, Pepí, and I were born in New York City.

When Daddy comes home from work we play our favorite sport, baseball. It's hard to catch the ball when I wear my heavy winter jacket. Last winter Mommy and Daddy took me to Puerto Rico for a vacation. I learned lots of things about my heritage.

Daddy grew up where there are palm trees, like in Florida. And it is warm every day in Puerto Rico, so warm that people can always play baseball without a jacket. Everyone in Puerto Rico speaks Spanish, just like my grandparents.

In our home we speak two languages, English and Spanish. Even Pepí speaks English and Spanish. My friends, Irma and Glen, speak Spanish, too. They come from another island called the Dominican Republic. If you come from a place where the people speak Spanish, you are called a Hispanic. We call ourselves Hispanic Americans because part of us is Spanish and part of us is American. In my city, there are lots of Hispanics from many different countries, but they all speak the same language, Spanish.

Sometimes Irma and Glen stop by to help me with my chores. We clean beans, then set them in a pot of water overnight to make them soft. Then Mommy shows me how to crush garlic for *sofrito* (so-frée-to), which is a mixture of Spanish spices that will go into the bean pot.

The next night, Mommy, Daddy, and I have our favorite dinner, *arroz con pollo y habichuelas* (a-rós kom bóy-jo ee a-bich-wél-as). It's rice with chicken and beans. Mommy and I are good cooks.

When my parents are at work, my mommy's mommy, Nana Carmen, takes me shopping at the *carniceria* (kar-nees-eriá, rhymes with Maria), the Spanish meat market. I get to pay.

"*Muchas gracias*" (móo-chas gráss-ee-as), the grocer says to thank me.

To answer, I say, "*De nada*" (day natha), which means "don't mention it."

My nana Carmen visits me every single day. At bedtime she comes to our home just to kiss me good-night. Sometimes she shows me her tiny hurts so I can tell her my special Spanish healing poem:

Sana, sana, sana, (sah-na)	Heal, heal, heal,
Si no te curas (see no tay kóoras) hoy, (oy)	If you don't heal today,
Te curas (tay kóoras) mañana. (man-yá-na)	You'll heal tomorrow.

Then I say my prayers to my guardian angel just like my mommy and daddy did when they were little. Nana Carmen says the guardian angel watches over children and keeps them safe while they sleep.

When Mommy is home from work, she plays Spanish music on the stereo. Then my friends, Mommy, and I dance the *merengue* (me-rén-gay). When we hear the music we shake our hips and move to the beat: one-two, one-two. In Spanish we count like this: *uno* (oono), *dos* (sounds almost like toast).

In my family, next to baseball, we love Spanish dances best. When my *madrina* (ma-dree-na), that's my godmother, stops in for a visit, she dances with us. Sometimes Daddy, Nana Carmen, and my friends' mommy join in. And Pepí sings, "*¡MERENGUE!*"

欽

Admire

蘭

Orchid

My name in America is April. I also have a Chinese name: *Chin* (ching), which means "admire" and *Lan* (lan), which means "orchid."

Both my parents are Chinese and were born in Taiwan. Taiwan is an island on the other side of the world. My papa came to New York without his parents to go to school and my mama moved here with her family. Because Julius, my older brother, and May, my older sister, and I were born in America, we are called Chinese Americans.

There are many Chinese Americans. But we do not all speak the same Chinese language. The way my family speaks Chinese is called Mandarin.

In Mandarin, I call my daddy *baba* (bah-bah) and my mommy *mama* (mah-mah). It sounds something like English, but when we write the words they look very different. Another thing that's different in Chinese is that words aren't made with letters. Each word has its own special marks.

爸
爸

Father

媽
媽

Mother

During the week we go to public school, but on Saturday we go to Chinese school. There we learn how to speak and write in Chinese, like my parents learned in Taiwan. When I write English letters, I write from the left side of the page to the right. When I write in Chinese, I write from the right to the left. And I write in rows from the top of the page to the bottom. For us Chinese-American kids there are many things to remember.

In Chinese school we also learn a special kind of writing called calligraphy. We use a brush instead of a pen, black ink, and special paper made from stalks of rice. Our teacher shows us the right way to hold the brush.

芝
蔴
涼
麵

Cold Sesame
Noodles

My favorite part of Chinese school is snack time. Today, Mama made me cold sesame noodles, *tsu ma liang mein* (tsu mah leeang mee-en). I eat them with a fork, but most Chinese people eat their noodles with chopsticks. I'm just learning to eat with chopsticks.

Papa told us that an Italian explorer named Marco Polo discovered noodles in China a long time ago and introduced them to his country.

When Mama brought home takeout, Julius asked if a Chinese explorer discovered pizza in Italy.

Mama and Papa laughed and said, "No."

While we eat our pizza we play a game to test our wits. Papa asks us to look for letters hidden in the picture on the pizza box. Julius sees a *V* in the pizza man's shoe. May finds an *L*.

Oh, look! I can even see the Chinese letter *Ba* (bah), in the pizza man's eyebrows. *Ba* means "eight" in Chinese.

八

Eight

七巧板

Chi chiao
bang

At night when we have finished all our chores and all our homework, we play *Chi chiao bang* (chee chow bang). In America some people call it Tangram. This is a popular game in Taiwan, like checkers is in America. My grandparents and even my great-grandparents played this game. To play, you move seven different shapes to build a new shape. I like to make a pussycat. It is very difficult, but I can do it. Papa says, "Go slowly and think about a cat. After a while your mind will start to run and you will see the cat in the shapes." He's right.

There is an old Chinese saying, "The older you are the wiser you become." When I become a grown-up, I will remember to tell this to my family.

THE THINGS WE EAT

SANU'S
TIEBOU DIENN
(6 servings)

The fish and paste:
2 stalks celery
1 bunch fresh parsley
2 large yellow onions
2 tbs. soy sauce
4-6 cloves garlic
1 tsp. salt
3–4 lbs. whole thick white fish
oil for frying

The stew:
2-3 onions, finely chopped
3 tbs. soy sauce
4 oz. tomato paste
4 carrots
1 heaping tbs. black pepper
1 small cabbage
2 med. eggplants
2 yams
2 potatoes or cassavas
3-4 chili peppers
3 cups uncooked rice

In a blender, combine all the fish and paste ingredients, except the fish and oil (or chop these ingredients together). Cut deep slits into the fish and stuff the combined ingredients into the pockets and in the insides. Put 2 to 3 inches of oil into a large skillet and fry the fish until golden. Remove and drain. Pour all but 3 tbs. of oil out of pan. Add the onion, soy sauce, tomato paste, and 6 cups of water. Chop the stew vegetables into large chunks and stir all the vegetables and the black pepper into the skillet. Cook over medium heat until tender. During the last few minutes of cooking, add the fish. Remove the fish and vegetables to a heat-proof platter. When the fish is cool enough to touch, cut it into bite-size pieces, removing all bones. Measure the water left in the skillet, leaving 6 cups of liquid. Add rice and cook. To assemble, place the rice in a large bowl. Spread fish and vegetables evenly on top. (Remember to wash your hands before eating.)

ERIC'S HABICHUELAS
(4 servings)

½ lb. small dried red beans
1 tbs. sofrito*
1 can tomato sauce
1 bunch culantro (or cilantro)
2 green peppers, chopped

Soak beans in 4 cups of cold water overnight. Bring beans to a boil. Pour out and add another 4 cups cold water and boil again. Cook until tender. Add water if necessary. Add *sofrito*, tomato sauce, green peppers, and chopped culantro to the pot. Cover and simmer about 20 minutes.
**sofrito* is made up of crushed garlic, onions, tomato paste, oil, coriander, and salt. It can be found in supermarkets where Spanish foods are sold.

APRIL'S COLD SESAME NOODLES
(1 serving)

2 oz. cooked Chinese noodles or spaghetti
1 tbs. sesame sauce or peanut butter
1 tsp. soy sauce
1 tsp. chopped scallion

In a bowl mix the sesame sauce (or peanut butter) with 1 tbs. warm water and soy sauce. Add to the cooked, cooled noodles and sprinkle scallion on top. Stir before eating.

...And Pepí gets the chicken bone.

AUTHOR'S NOTE

My series of photo essays for young children grew out of my long-standing interest in how various people confront situations over which they have no control. I began the series with familiar situations that most children face—going to the doctor and going to the dentist. I design my books to be personal and closeup. What most intrigues me are the children's feelings and their understanding of these settings and experiences. And so I ask them.

The children are more than willing to share their thoughts and have much to tell me. They like the idea that other children their age will benefit from their insights. This is true for all my books.

Each photo essay has a dual purpose: to explain a common event to a child in a child's terms and to present a model of an experience—be it nursery school or gymnastics class—to the adult world. In this book, I wanted to show how families impart a sense of identity to their young children. I intentionally chose families with at least one foot in another country to highlight the conscious choices a family must make in everyday activities to perpetuate a sense of heritage.

Before I began this project, I hoped to create a book that simultaneously celebrated differences and recognized similarities. Once I spent time with the three families, it became clear their real lives satisfied these goals.

Sanu, Eric, and April took great pride in teaching me about who they are and what makes their families distinctive. It has been a joy to know them.